P9-CMD-683

SEEING
IN SPECIAL WAYS

CHILDREN LIVING WITH BLINDNESS

DON'T
TURN
AWAY

For a free color catalog describing Gareth Stevens' list of high-quality children's books call 1-800-433-0942.

Library of Congress Cataloging-in-Publication Data

Bergman, Thomas, 1947-
    Seeing in special ways--children living with blindness.

    (Don't turn away)
    Translation of: Fingrar som ser.
    Summary: Interviews with a group of blind and partially sighted children in Sweden reveal their feelings about their disability and the ways they use their other senses to help them "see."
    1. Children, Blind--Juvenile literature. [1. Blind. 2. Visually handicapped. 3. Physically handicapped] I. Title. II. Series.
HV1596.3.B4713   1988   362.4'1'088054   88-42970
ISBN 1-55532-915-2

D O N 'T
T U R N
A W A Y

North American edition first published in 1989 by

Gareth Stevens, Inc.
7317 West Green Tree Road
Milwaukee, Wisconsin 53223, USA

First published in Swedish in 1976 by LiberFörlag under the title *Fingrar som ser*.

Series Editor: MaryLee Knowlton
Research Editor: Scott Enk
Series Designer: Kate Kriege

Printed in the United States of America

1 2 3 4 5 6 7 8 9 9 95 94 93 92 91 90 89

SEEING
IN SPECIAL WAYS

CHILDREN LIVING WITH BLINDNESS

DON'T
TURN
AWAY

Thomas Bergman

Gareth Stevens Children's Books
MILWAUKEE

When Thomas Bergman first showed me the remarkable photographs that appear in Seeing in Special Ways, I was struck by their power to capture the essence of children's personalities and moods. As we looked at them together — I for the first time, he once again after many times — I was moved by the intensity and passion of a person who cares deeply about children who are blind.

Thomas is Sweden's best-known children's photographer, with a reputation stretching from Europe to Japan. His compassion, admiration, and affection for children with disabilities inspired him to embark on a special photographic mission. The striking black-and-white photographs you will see in this book will remain in your memory. The thoughts and feelings that Thomas' young friends have shared with him form the basis for the insightful text that accompanies the pictures.

You will meet children in the pages of this book with a disability that may be unfamiliar to you. You will be inspired by the originality and courage with which they meet the challenges presented by this disability. And you will be moved by the many ways that they are like children everywhere. I hope you will ask yourself, as I did, "Why haven't I met many children like these? Where are they? Why don't I see them in the schools and on playgrounds, in museums and shopping malls, on the streets and in the parks?" These are the questions we must explore. Our communities should embrace all people. We will all be the richer for it.

In Seeing in Special Ways, Andrew, Katie, George, and other remarkable children show us that a disability should not be a cause for embarrassment, separation, and fear. Instead, it should be a reason for reaching out, sharing the joys, sorrows, and hopes of our lives.

Gareth Stevens

Gareth Stevens
PUBLISHER

*T*he children in this book are students at the Tomteboda School for the Blind in Stockholm, Sweden. As you read our conversations and look at their pictures, you will come to understand how they see themselves and the world and their place in it.

I felt hesitant at first about photographing children with impaired sight who would never be able to see or approve my pictures. Most of the children, though, were quite happy about it, telling me, "We think you ought to put cameras in every corner and photograph us in every situation." They helped me choose the situations and settings to be photographed. Their fantasies about their pictures influenced my work and ideas of how they saw themselves.

Because I am a photographer, I thought of myself as especially observant of my surroundings. But these children taught me new ways of seeing, both as a photographer and as a human being.

I've learned how to see a face with my fingers as they do, feeling where the nose is, what the eyes and ears are like, how soft the cheeks and lips are, how thick or curly the hair. It is a new way of knowing a friend, and these children are my friends.

I want to thank the children of Tomteboda School, and I dedicate this book to them. It is their creation as much as it is mine.

Thomas Bergman

Thomas Bergman

ANDREW
9 years old

I can cane-walk.

Thomas: Is the stick a great help to you?

Andrew: Yes. It's just like a long finger. I can see with it — because if I am going to bump into anything, the cane tells me. I feel with it before each step. I swing it from side to side and when I put my right foot forward, the cane is on the opposite side, on the left checking out what lies ahead.

Thomas: What do you like to do best of all?

Andrew: I like to touch cars and feel them and sit in them. Real cars, I mean.

Thomas: How do you feel a car?

Andrew: Well, I touch it all around and feel what sort of shape it is and where the lights are. And I like to sit in it and start it and pretend to drive it. And I usually ask what color it is — I like colors a lot. My favorite colors are blue, orange, red, yellow, and green. I really like all colors — and silver, too.

Thomas: Do you think you will ever be able to drive a car?

Andrew: Maybe, if they can do something about my eye.

Thomas: Have they told you that they can?

Andrew: No, they haven't operated on it. I won't be allowed to take a driving test unless my eye is all right.

Thomas: Do you hope that you'll be able to drive one day?

Andrew: Yes, I do. But I don't suppose I ever will.

Thomas: Do you dream about being able to see?

Andrew: Yes, I dream about it sometimes. At night I lie in bed and dream about driving a car.

Thomas: And where do you drive?

Andrew: Oh, all over the place.

Thomas: **Do you like touching my cameras?**

Andrew: Yes, it's super. I wouldn't know what you were doing otherwise.

Thomas: **How do you feel about my taking pictures of you?**

Andrew: Fine, especially since you've told me what you're doing.

Thomas: **Do you think I can take good pictures of you?**

Andrew: Yes, I do, but some of them may go wrong, though. Tell me, is this the right way to hold a camera?

Thomas: **Yes, it is. If you were me, how would you do it?**

Andrew: I would put up cameras everywhere, in every room and on every wall. Every window and wall.

Thomas: **Why?**

Andrew: Well, you'd be able to take pictures of us all the time, whenever you wanted to, wouldn't you?

Thomas: **You want to show yourselves in every situation, do you?**

Andrew: Yes, just as we are. And there ought to be a bucket for developing the pictures so we could have them at once.

Thomas: **Could you tell me how you lost your sight?**

Andrew: My mother had German measles when I was born, and that made me go blind. I could see a little with my right eye and almost nothing with my left. Then, when I was six years old, I was playing in my room and I wanted to get a microphone from another room. I rushed out and banged right into the door, and the doorknob went right into my eye and the eye broke. Everything went dark and I saw stars exploding all around me and I was very frightened. But I didn't cry much.

Thomas: **Was your mother at home at the time?**

Andrew: Yes, and she was very upset. I was upset, too, just a little. I had a friend with me — he was scared, I think.

Thomas: **Were you terribly disappointed that you couldn't see any more?**

Andrew: Well, yes. When I got to the hospital they operated on my eye. And they said that they might be able to do something for me, but it didn't work. All I can see now is darkness and light.

Thomas: **Do you sometimes think about your blindness?**

Andrew: No, not very often. I take it as it is. I'm so used to it.

Thomas: **Sighted children go to ordinary schools and live at home with their mothers and fathers. But you have to go to boarding school. Tell me what it feels like to be away from your mother and father and your little sister for so long.**

Andrew: Well, I'm used to it, because I had to stay in the hospital for such a long time. I was homesick the first year, though.

Thomas: **Would you rather go to a school for sighted children if you could?**

Andrew: Oh, yes, because then I'd be able to live at home.

Thomas: **There are twenty-one of you here, and you have to be together all the time, night and day. How do you get along with each other?**

Andrew: We get along fine. I have lots of friends here.

11

Thomas: **You've got a little sister who is five years old, haven't you?**

Andrew: Yes. Her name is Asa and she isn't blind. She shows me things and helps me quite a lot. But sometimes she gets impatient with me and runs off!

Thomas: **Do you think your parents behave differently toward you and your sister?**

Andrew: They help me more with some things, I guess, but I don't think I need much help, really.

Thomas: **Is there anything you miss?**

Andrew: Yes, I would like to see. When I ride my bike, for instance, I have to know the road or I can't pedal. I have to push with my feet instead. Going downhill — you know, when the road isn't straight or uphill — I can't pedal at all. I have to feel the road with my feet. But if I could see, I could ride on roads that I don't know.

Thomas: **When you are older you may meet a girl that you like. What do you think will make you like her? Do you think looks are important?**

Andrew: Well, a little, maybe. But mostly I'll like her because she's good company.

Thomas: **Will she have to help you, do you think?**

Andrew: I suppose so. With a few things I can't do myself.

Thomas: **Would you like her to be able to see?**

Andrew: No, that wouldn't matter at all.

Thomas: **What sort of work would you like to do?**

Andrew: Work? Well, I don't really know. I keep changing my mind. Sometimes I want to be a baker, and sometimes I want to work in a shop selling organs. But mostly I want to be a baker, because they have to start very early in the morning.

Thomas: **You like getting up early?**

Andrew: Yes, because I usually wake up at four-thirty.

Thomas: **Do you think we grown-ups are too fussy and smothering because you can't see? Does it irritate you when we try to help you with things that you can do yourself?**

Andrew: Well, sometimes I think, "I can manage myself," and I say so. They don't always understand, though.

12

Thomas: **How do you see your future, Andrew?**

Andrew: I believe in the future. I think life is fun!

KATIE

9 years old

When I was born I weighed as much as a pound of butter.

Katie: I'm Katie. When I was born I weighed as much as a pound of butter, and I was no bigger than a can of beer. Well, maybe about half an inch longer! I was born three months too early and I had to be in an oxygen tent for a long time.

Thomas: Is that why you can't see?

Katie: Yes. There were tubes that let out oxygen, and lots of other things. That's why I went blind. I had too much oxygen in my eyes when I was lying there. The doctor said, "She's going to die." But I didn't die, did I? Because I'm still alive!

Thomas: They really thought you would die?

Katie: Yes, because I was so tiny.

Thomas: How much can you see? Can you see colors?

Katie: My best colors are stripes and squares.

Thomas: And what colors are they?

Katie: It doesn't really matter. Red or green or blue or yellow.

Thomas: What's the hardest thing of all for you?

Katie: I can't do as much as children who can see. I can't run as fast because I'm afraid of bumping into things, and I can't cross the street. Children who can see know when a car is coming. But anyway, people shouldn't play in the street, should they? Some of them do, though.

Thomas: **Do you think that you're not good at doing things because you can't see properly?**

Katie: Yes. Some people make me feel that. I don't know why, but sometimes I feel stupid when I'm with children who can see. They tease me and make fun.

Thomas: **Can you look at yourself in the mirror and see what you look like?**

Katie: Yes, but I can't stare into my own eyes. If I do, everything goes black.

Thomas: **What do you think grown-ups can do to help blind children?**

Katie: Well, I don't think cars should drive any old way. Just think what would happen if you were going along and you tried to cross the road and a car came along at full speed and didn't notice that a child was crossing. I worry that in stores people might cheat me and give me the wrong change. I cut my bangs myself. Give me your hand, Matthew, and you can feel how they turned out.

GEORGE A.
8 years old

I would like to feel the pictures on TV.

Thomas: **How do you find each other when you play tag?**

George: When I'm "It," I shout, "I'm 'It!' Look out!"

Andrew: And I shout, "I'm here, I'm here!"

Thomas: **So your hearing is very important?**

George: Yes, it's important, because when I can hear, I go on searching until I find him. I know he's here someplace.

Thomas: **Tell me what you do to find out what each of you looks like.**

George: Well, when Andrew touches my face he can feel that my nose is a long way down and my eyes are deep-set, and that's how he knows that's me.

Thomas: **Will you show me how you do some things for yourself?**

George: Sure. Watch how I pour milk. I just put my finger in the glass and pour out the milk with the other hand. Then I can feel with the tip of my finger when the glass is about half-full, and I can easily tell when it's quite full.

Thomas: **Is it hard for you to do certain things?**

George: Yes, it's hard to run so you don't bump into the table in the corridor and knock it over as I did once. The table crashed to the floor and made a terrible noise. And when I ride a bike, I could ride right into a car. So I can't ever ride where there's traffic.

Thomas: **Is there anything you can do better than children who can see?**

George: Some things. For instance, if I make a mistake when I read Braille, nobody else knows, so they can't tease me, can they? Because only blind people can read Braille — at least, that's what I've been told, but I don't know for sure, so I'd better go into town and ask everybody I meet in the street! I taught a friend of mine to read Braille, you know.

Thomas: **What would you like to do most?**

George: I'd like to drive a bus when I grow up.

Thomas: **Do you think you'll ever be able to do that?**

George: No, I don't think so. You have to be able to see to drive a bus.

Thomas: **Is that what you want most of all? Would you like to be able to see?**

George: Yes, very much.

Thomas: **Can you see pictures?**

George: I'd like to see the pictures on television — I'd like that very much. I'd like to feel the pictures. They should make a television where you can feel the pictures.

Thomas: **Do you see any shapes or forms inside your head at all?**

George: *Yes*, I do. I can see a monster in the ceiling.

Thomas: **When do you see that?**

George: I see it when I think about it. I can see the monster whenever I want to.

Thomas: **What does it look like?**

George: It looks like a big man with horrible arms and a huge mouth.

Thomas: **What does it feel like to live at school?**

George: Not good. I get homesick.

TODD AND KATHERINE

both 9 years old

He talks funny, but I think he's very cute.

Katherine: I don't know why I'm blind. There was something wrong with my mother when she had me.

Todd: There was something wrong with my mother, too, so I'm a bit blind.

Thomas: **You both have defective sight?**

Todd: Yes, I have. A little.

Katherine: But we're not really blind.

Thomas: **What do you like best of all, Katherine?**

Katherine: Playing with Todd! And listening to records.

Todd: I like riding my bike and swinging on a swing and riding a scooter and running down the corridors to the dining room and playing tricks on people. That's great fun!

Katherine I'm going to marry Todd. We're going to get married, aren't we, Todd? Tell Thomas.

Todd: We are. We really are, because we're in love.

Katherine: Todd, do you want to marry me? I want to marry you.

Todd: Oh, yes, I'd like to get married.

Katherine: I like him. I think he's cute. He talks funny, but I think he's very cute!

Thomas: **How can a castanet help you understand what you're hearing?**

Todd: I can hear that castanets have many different sounds, not just one. We are learning to tell what sounds mean and where they come from. I know who you are by the sound of your walk. I know it's you, Thomas. I must learn to understand the sounds of the street.

PETER

7 years old

There should be a mirror where you can feel what you look like.

Peter: I was three years old when I went blind, but I think I want to stay blind.

Thomas: **Why is that?**

Peter: Well, I'm used to it now. I'm seven years old. The only bad thing about it is that I can't go out on my own. If I could see, I could get a good job and walk to work myself, or drive a car.

Thomas: **Do you worry about things like that already?**

Peter: No, not really. I just talk about it.

Thomas: **Do you know what you look like, Peter?**

Peter: No. Well, yes, in a way I do. I've cut out the shapes of my head and feet and hands and felt the pictures.

Thomas: **Why do you think that people who can see look at themselves in the mirror?**

Peter: Because they want to know what they look like. There should be a mirror where you can feel what you look like. But there isn't, is there?

Can't you tell them to make one? And I think there ought to be more "bleepers" to help you cross the street. Grown-ups aren't at all considerate.

Thomas: **Do you watch television?**

Peter: Well, yes, a bit, but I think people who work in television are silly. Can't you tell them to have more talking? More shows with lots and lots of talking.

Thomas: **How do you feel about being photographed when you won't be able to see the pictures I take?**

Peter: I think it's super. And you've told me about the pictures you're going to use in the book and I think that's fine.

Thomas: **Do you think things are a lot easier for children who can see than they are for you?**

Peter: Yes, because they can go out on their own. And they don't have to go to boarding school.

Thomas: Why do you think you have to go to boarding school?

Peter: Because there aren't so many blind children.

Thomas: What are your friends at home like, the ones that can see?

Peter: They're okay. Sometimes they cheat but there's no need to feel sorry for me.

Thomas: Do you think you're better at some things than children who can see?

Peter: Yes, I can feel things with my fingers better than they can, and I can hear much better, and I can smell flowers and things like that. I can taste better, too, but I can't think of anything in particular just now.

Thomas: Are you scared of the dark, Peter?

Peter: No, I'm not. I can turn out the light and cover my eyes and I'm not a bit scared.

Thomas: Do you like colors?

Peter: Yes, nearly all of them. Blue, violet, orange, green. But they look darker and different from when I could see. Some of them are a bit lighter dark, and some are quite light. I remember what the colors look like.

Thomas: Do you see any shapes or pictures in your mind? Just before you go to sleep, for instance?

Peter: Yes, that's when I think about lots of different things, and things that have happened to me.

Thomas: When you are in a place where you have never been before, do you wonder what it looks like?

Peter: Yes, but I still think it's great being there. And I think it's great to fly in an airplane when I go home.

Thomas: If you could wish for something, what would it be?

Peter: I would like a guide dog, a Labrador, but I won't get one until I am grown up.

26

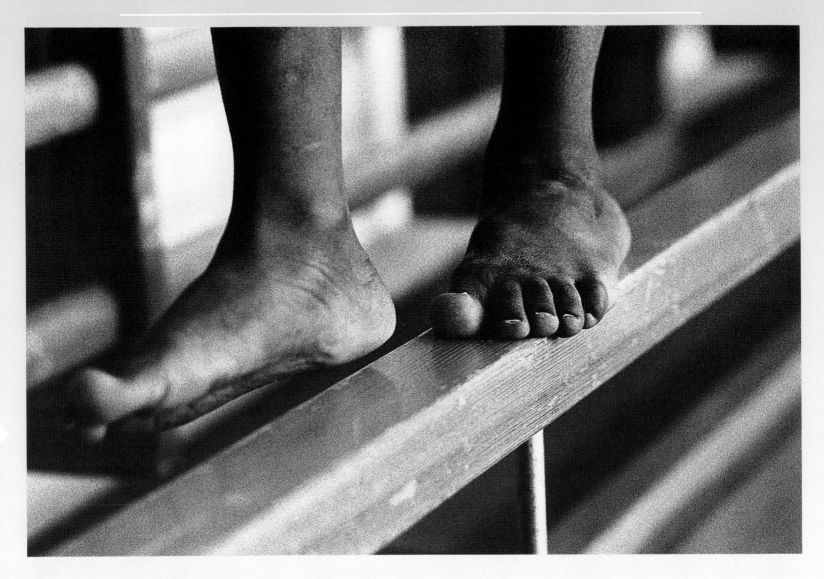

Thomas: **Is balancing on the bar useful, do you think?**

Peter: Since I've been practicing on it, I can run faster when I play. And I can run up and down the stairs. I like to move fast.

31

Thomas: **Can you read and write?**

Peter: Well, of course. I can write two
ways. One with this Braille
machine. I think in letters and it
punches out Braille so my friends
can read what I've written. And so
can I. I practice my spelling with
these Braille blocks.

Thomas: **Your teacher has put different kinds of vegetables in a cup with water so you cannot smell it. You can only taste it.**

You must tell what each vegetable is just by tasting and touching it with your tongue. What does it taste like?

Peter: I will try to fish up the vegetable with my tongue. Ach! It's an onion. It's awful. I'll try to get another one.

Thomas: **How can you tell what kind of animal this is?**

Peter: First I see a picture in my mind of what the animal looks like. But I really don't know what it looks like. I touch and hold it first. I hold the head first and feel for the nose. Then I touch the body all over to see how big it is. Oh! It's a rabbit. I feel it because its feet are big and so are its ears. I also smell it.

JOHN
7 years old

I would like to fly to the moon and play the piano.

Thomas: **Have you ever been able to see?**

John: I think that once when I was very small, I could see. When you and I didn't know each other. But I've always been able to play the piano.

Thomas: **Which instrument do you like best?**

John: A honky-tonk piano. I've heard them but I've never played one.

Thomas: **What would you like to be when you're grown up?**

John: Three things: a piano tuner, a drummer, and a pianist. But I think it'll be too difficult to be a piano tuner because then I'd have to drive a car, and I can't see, so that won't work.

Thomas: **Can't you see anything at all, John?**

John: No. I can only see colors and light and darkness. The light things are quite smooth and all the dark things are rough.

Thomas: **Do you see pictures, John, and can you visualize this room?**

John: Yes, the piano and everything.

Thomas: **What colors do you like?**

John: Orange, yellow, blue, white, and bright yellow.

Thomas: **Are you scared of the dark?**

John: I don't know what you mean.

Thomas: **Are you afraid of things that you imagine are hiding in the dark? Horrible old men, or monsters?**

John: No, I've never seen anything like that.

Thomas: **Sometimes you're so quiet. What do you think about when you're so quiet?**

John: I was wondering today where all the yesterdays go. Do you know, Thomas? Where do they go? I feel sorry for all those days, just disappearing. Maybe they fly up to the moon!

KENT

11 years old

My dream is to be a technologist and mend cassettes.

Thomas: **How long have you been here at Tomteboda School? Why are you here?**

Kent: Because I've got impaired vision. I've been here for four years.

Thomas: **Is it difficult being at a boarding school?**

Kent: Yes, especially when you have to sleep by yourself.

Thomas: **Why do you sleep by yourself?**

Kent: Because Andrew and I used to talk until nine o'clock every night and that made Andrew tired in the daytime. You see, we have to go to bed at eight, but I'm never tired then.

Thomas: **Are you homesick?**

Kent: No, I'm not. I think it's silly to be homesick.

Thomas: **If you could wish for something, what would it be?**

Kent: My dream is to be a technologist and mend cassettes. I like playing and listening to children's radio and reading.

Thomas: **Do you think you'll be blind all your life?**

Kent: Yes. I had too much oxygen when I was a baby and it destroyed my eyes.

Thomas: **Can you see any shapes and forms, Kent?**

Kent: I see a lot of black shadows, and at night I see black men running around in the room. I call them dreams.

Thomas: Do you like colors?

Kent: Yes, blue. I like looking at colors because I'm not colorblind.

Thomas: How does it feel to be photographed when you won't be able to see the pictures I take of you?

Kent: Horrid, because I don't know what I look like.

Thomas: Do you want to know what you look like?

Kent: Oh, yes!

Thomas: Is there something that you would specially like to do but can't because you're blind?

Kent: I would like to look at television properly because the pictures just go round and round for me now. And I would like the programs to have more talk.

Thomas: How do you think grown-ups could improve things for you?

Kent: I think there should be more schools for the blind all over the country so that people could go home every weekend, preferably every day, and then I could live at home. And then there should be many more "bleepers" in the streets, so we can cross.

Thomas: What sort of difficulties do you come up against with your impaired vision?

Kent: Well, when I run, I often bump into walls and doors and things, so my mother has taken off the kitchen door at home.

Thomas: Is there anything you think you can do better than sighted children can?

Kent: Yes, I can read Braille. And I can tell with my fingers what things are. They can't do that.

39

Thomas: **What are your friends at home like? The ones that can see?**

Kent: Some of them are all right and we have a good time. But the big boys in my neighborhood sometimes pick on me.

Thomas: **And how do you feel then?**

Kent: I feel stupid and then I get angry. I try to tell myself that being cruel is their problem, not mine. But I don't always believe it. To have a friend is important, but I really don't have one.

JORDAN
9 years old

*I always have to make up a picture in my
mind about things, even in daylight.*

Jordan: I was born with one blind eye and
then, when I was in the hospital,
they fiddled around with the other
eye, and I went blind in that one too.
I was about three years old then.
And I had artificial eyes that I had
to change all the time. But one day
we noticed that the left eye didn't
fit. It was too large. The eye socket
had shrunk so I couldn't get it in.
So we went to Denmark. Dr.
Muller made a new artificial eye
that was quite different. And he
changed the other eye as well. I
don't really know why, but I had a
lot of radiation treatment, and
that's why this eye is so hollow.

Thomas: **Do you like TV?**

Jordan: Well, it doesn't do much for me. Why can't they do programs we can understand? When the television people ask what people want, they only ask those who can see.

Thomas: **How does that make you feel?**

Jordan: It makes me unhappy. I feel left out of the world sometimes. I also think that there ought to be more vacation tours for us and not just for grown-ups. When you're as young as I am, it's not easy to get about. I would like there to be many, many more vacation arrangements for us and not just for people who can see. We feel so isolated. We can't go out and play as we like.

Thomas: **Can't you ever play outside on your own?**

Jordan: No, only when I ride my bike in our yard, and it's not much fun just riding around and around by yourself. I like being indoors where I can listen to records and tapes.

Thomas: **Have you any friends you can go out with, or aren't you allowed out on your own with them?**

Jordan: No, but sometimes I call some of the boys I was at day care with before I came here and we talk. But not very often any more. And then I have a few pen pals. And there

was Frederick. He was nice. He used to spend his days with a baby-sitter next door and he came over to play with me a lot. But then the baby-sitter said that if he didn't spend all his time with her own kid, she wouldn't take care of him any more. So now I have nobody to play with.

Thomas: **Do you feel unsure of yourself when you are with friends who can see?**

Jordan: Not really, but, of course, I can't do everything they can. Like my friend Michael. He isn't much fun because he never wants to do anything that I can do too. He just wants to run up and down the street all the time.

Thomas: **Does he understand that you can't do that?**

Jordan: Well, yes, I suppose he does. But it doesn't really seem to matter to him. I think I need a better friend than Michael.

Thomas: **What do you think you are good at?**

Jordan: Well, I can swim quite well. And in a way it's not so bad being blind. For instance, you can't get scared of things in the dark, because you never know when it is dark! You can see pictures inside your head, of course, but they're not really frightening.

43

Thomas: Do you see pictures sometimes?

Jordan: Inside my head, yes. All the time.

Thomas: What kind of pictures?

Jordan: Well, what the classroom looks like, and that sort of thing.

Thomas: You were able to see at one time, weren't you?

Jordan: Yes, but when I could see, there were lots of things I never saw. You can't get around to everything before you're three years old, you know. But now when I get to a new place, a picture comes into my head and it's just as if I could see. But if I can't find my way, then no pictures come and the things get blurred.

Thomas: How do you see a person?

Jordan: Well, that's difficult to describe. It changes a lot, rather like the colors I see inside my head. It's very strange, but I do see some sort of picture.

Thomas: You miss some things, don't you? And you would like to see, wouldn't you?

Jordan: Sometimes. But if they could just improve television a little and give us some more things to do when we're not in school, I wouldn't have to go on wishing I could see all the time. And then some people make fun of me.

Thomas: Have you actually heard them do that? How do you react then?

Jordan: Well, it makes me very angry and unhappy, but I can't chase them, can I? I want to beat them up and show them that I can look after myself as well as they can. There are lots of things that we can do that they can't, but people won't believe us. We run around at Tomteboda just as much as children do anywhere.

Thomas: Don't you think that they only say things like that because they're ignorant?

Jordan: Yes, but I still don't think they ought to go around calling me names and running off just because I can't get at them. I've learned to find my way around here at Tomteboda, and I can run as much as I like. If I hadn't learned that, I wouldn't be able to do anything, would I?

Thomas: Children who can see are afraid of the dark. You know that, don't you?

Jordan: Yes, because they're used to seeing everything and when it's dark and they can't recognize things, they get scared and start imagining all sorts of things. But I don't imagine anything horrible when I don't recognize things, because I can't ever see anything around me. I always have to make up a picture in my mind about things, even in daylight.

Thomas: You said that you can see colors. Which colors do you like best?

Jordan: Yellow and green. But I am not very interested in what color my clothes are. I don't think it's very important.

45

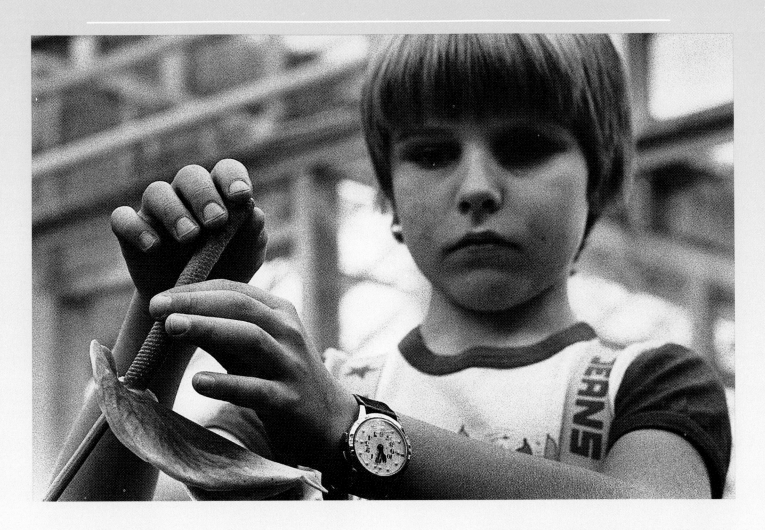

46

Thomas: **How do you know what kind of flower this is?**

Jordan: I use my index fingers and my fingertips to feel the details of the flower, and then I can tell what kind it is.

I like the summer best because that's when the flowers bloom, and with some I can tell what kind it is just by smelling. But to be able to smell the same kind of flower-smells in the city — well, the city has to change! And I think that people ought to be better informed about disabilities. They lost their heads and try to help us too much, and that doesn't bring any useful changes, does it? But I don't want to sit imprisoned in a corner with everybody rushing past without having time to stop and listen. When I grow up I'm going to fight for the blind children who will be growing up then, and see to it that they get a better city to live in. And a chance to go to a day school so they can live at home.

QUESTIONS FROM CHILDREN ABOUT BLINDNESS

*Q*uestions in your mind can keep you from feeling comfortable about being around people with disabilities. Here are some answers to questions children often ask about being blind.

What does it mean to say someone is blind?
There is a legal definition for blindness. It says that people are legally blind (1) if they can see less at 20 feet (6 m) than a person with normal vision sees at 200 feet (61 m) or (2) if they cannot see to the sides, if they have what is usually called "tunnel vision."

Can legally blind people see anything at all?
Most people who are legally blind can see something. Some see light or colors. Others see large objects or moving objects. Others see things straight in front of them or things to the side of them.

Can blind people hear better than sighted people? Can they feel colors?
No, they can't. A blind person's other senses are no different than anyone else's. However, blind people train themselves to use these senses because they need them more than a sighted person does. If you close your eyes, you will probably feel more in touch with what your ears can tell you. At night, you are more sensitive to sounds and what they mean because your eyes don't tell you as much as they do when it's light. You also pay more attention to what you smell and feel when you can't see.

How does a person read Braille?
Braille is a method of reading by touch. It was developed in 1824 by a French inventor, teacher, and musician named Louis Braille. He had been blind since he was three. Braille is a system of raised dots occupying six positions in a box shape known as a cell. With this system, all the letters, numbers, and punctuation of a language can be reproduced as raised dots on paper. These dots are read by a person's fingers as they pass over them. A person trained to read Braille can read about 100 words a minute, about half as many as an average sighted person reads with the eyes. Below is a picture of the position of the dots.

48

BRAILLE DIAGRAM

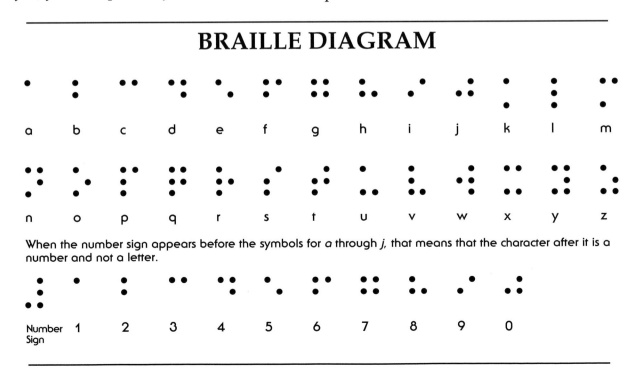

When the number sign appears before the symbols for *a* through *j*, that means that the character after it is a number and not a letter.

Braille books are bigger than print books. The paper is thicker and the Braille cells themselves take up more space than letters. Many blind people have a Braille writer that looks much like a typewriter. Some children have them at their desks at school for taking notes.

Are there other special aids for blind people?
Yes. For people who have some vision, there are large-print books in most libraries, TV screen enlargers, and magnifiers they can hold.

People who cannot use their eyes at all for reading have other ways to read. Talking Books are records or tapes that contain a whole book, speeded up to go faster than normal speech. Untrained people would have trouble absorbing information at this speed. Blind people are quite used to it. Talking computers are becoming more available and less expensive. More common is the Optacon, an older machine that translates printed material into electrical patterns that trained persons can read with their fingers.

There are Braille watches, Braille telephones, talking alarm clocks, talking scales, and key rings that beep when you clap your hands. But two of the most useful pieces of equipment for people with visual handicaps are ones sighted people rely on as well, the typewriter and the tape recorder.

What is a guide dog?
Guide dogs are specially trained dogs that take blind people many places they could not otherwise go safely. The dogs read traffic signals and recognize barriers. They can learn the daily routines of their owners and help them through these routines.

Guide dogs are allowed to go anywhere people who need them might go, including restaurants, grocery stores, movies, and planes, buses, and trains. They wear a harness you can easily spot; it is rectangular in shape and stiff. When you see a dog like this, remember that it has a job to do. Don't talk to a guide dog or pet it without asking its owner.

How is a guide dog trained?
Organized training programs for dogs and their owners have been available in North America since 1929. No one kind of dog is considered the best kind. But for size, dependability, and intelligence, the most common are Labradors, golden retrievers, German shepherds, Alsatians, and collies.

The first training a guide dog gets is in the home of a friendly family, usually one with children. The small puppy is temporarily placed in a home so it grows to young adulthood accustomed to being with people. If the dog proves to be patient and intelligent enough to be trained, it is sent to a special school for further training. There the dog learns what it will need to know in order to provide safe mobility for its owner.

The owner must be trained, too. A person seeking a guide dog will spend several weeks living at the guide dog school, learning how to keep a dog healthy, well-groomed, and disciplined. Each dog and each owner are unique, and they must learn to understand each other.

How does cane walking work?
A person who uses a cane for mobility will have one individually prescribed. Its length depends on the person's height and the length of the stride when walking. Generally it comes to the middle of the chest. The person waves the cane in an arc in front of the foot that is about to take a step, gently tapping to inspect the surface.

Only legally blind people can use a white cane, and they have special rights. Drivers must let them by regardless of the traffic light or stop sign.

. . . MORE QUESTIONS

What should I do when I meet a blind person?
Introduce yourself just the way you would to anyone else. Say something like, "I'm Karen Wasserman. I don't think we've met." If you have met the person before, say something like, "We met at Davey Fritz's house last month."

Talk in your normal speaking voice. Blind people are just as likely to hear well as you are and don't need to be shouted at. If the blind person is with someone else, don't ignore the blind person and talk only to the companion. This habit of sighted people is probably the most irritating of all to blind people.

What if something really stupid comes out of my mouth like, "I don't like the looks of this," or "Do you see what I mean?"
Don't worry about it. These phrases have more than one meaning and blind people use them, too. As you get to know someone better, you won't be so self-conscious, and you probably won't worry about these things.

What do I do if I see someone who needs help crossing the street?
First, be sure you're right. Ask blind persons if they want to cross and if you can help. Too many blind people tell of being dragged across the street by eager helpers who didn't think to ask if they wanted to cross. Just say, "Excuse me, do you want to cross the street? I can help." If the answer is yes, here is the way to provide physical assistance: Allow blind persons to take your arm. They will hold it just above your elbow and will walk just slightly behind you. Warn them of any changes in level or of water in the gutter or ice coming up. Use directional words like "left" and "right" rather than "over here" or "by this post."

How will I know if a blind person needs help?
Sometimes your common sense will tell you. A blind person whose groceries have just spilled all over needs help. Who wouldn't? Most often, blind people will ask for help if they need it just as anyone else would.

THINGS TO DO AND TALK ABOUT

Here are some simple things to do that will give you some idea of what it is like to be blind.

1. Blindfolded, try this: Find your shoes in your bedroom. Was it easy? Knowing the room as well as you do and (maybe) having a regular place to keep your shoes gives you a start. Blind people who want to be independent are probably more likely than you are to keep things where they belong so they can find them.

2. Pile all your socks together. Blindfolded, pick out the ones that will go with what you want to wear tomorrow. This isn't easy, is it? Without practice, you can't feel the patterns of the knit and you certainly can't find the right colors. Some people with visual handicaps make Braille labels for their clothes, labeling them by pattern and color so they can put outfits together.

3. Use a stick or umbrella to practice cane walking. Try it in the house, then in your yard. Where is it most useful? What difficulties do you encounter?

4. Try writing some Braille. Using the diagram on page 48 as a guide, do it first with a pen or pencil. Write your name. Then try a few words. Then try some stiff paper and a small nail. Punch holes in the paper with the nail, making the words you wrote earlier. Touch them. Can you read them? Braille reading takes time to learn, just like sighted reading.

5. Look for Braille in the buildings you go into. Check for Braille at elevators. Would a blind person be able to find the right bathroom? Where else do you think you might find Braille? Here's one hint: At some fast-food restaurants, run your fingers over the top of a drink cup. What do you feel? Which restaurants have Braille writing on their cups? Your library is a good source for Braille, too. Some even have Braille bookmarks.

51

WHERE TO WRITE FOR MORE INFORMATION

The people at the offices listed below will send you information about visual handicaps if you write to them. Many of them also have state and local branches as well as the national offices listed here. Check your phone book if you want to talk to someone locally. You may be able to call or go to an office in your hometown. When you write or call these people, tell them the reason for your interest so they can send you what will be most useful.

American Council of the Blind
1010 Vermont Avenue NW, Suite 1100
Washington, DC 20005

American Foundation for the Blind
15 West 16th Street
New York, NY 10011

American Library Association
Library Services for Exceptional Children
50 East Huron Street
Chicago, IL 60611

American Printing House for the Blind
P.O. Box 6085
1839 Frankfort Avenue
Louisville, KY 40206

Association for the Education and Rehabilitation
    of the Blind and Visually Impaired
206 N. Washington St., Suite 320
Alexandria, VA 22314

Canadian Council of the Blind
#510 220 Dundas Street
London, Ontario N6A 1H3

Canadian National Institute for the Blind
1931 Bayview Avenue
Toronto, Ontario M4G 4C8

Columbia Lighthouse for the Blind
1421 P Street NW
Washington, DC 20005

National Federation of the Blind
1800 Johnson St.
Baltimore, MD 21230

National Library Services for the Blind and
    Physically Handicapped
Library of Congress
1291 Taylor Street NW
Washington, DC 20542

MORE BOOKS FOR CHILDREN ABOUT VISUAL HANDICAPS

The books listed below are about children like you who are blind. Some are fiction and some are about real children with something to tell you. Look for them in your school and public libraries. If you cannot find the one you want, ask someone to order it for you.

Connie's New Eyes. Wolf (Lippincott Jr.)
Feeling Free. Sullivan (Addison-Wesley)
*Like It Is: Facts and Feelings About Handicaps
    from Kids Who Know.* Adams (Walker)
My Mother Is Blind. Reuter (Childrens Press)
The New Boy is Blind. Thomas (Messner)
The Seeing Summer. Eyerly (Archway)

*Seeing Through the Dark: Blind and Sighted,
    A Vision Shared.* Weiss (Harcourt Brace
    Jovanovich)
Through Grandpa's Eyes. MacLachlan
    (Harper Jr.)
What If You Couldn't . . . ? A Book About Special Needs.
    Kamien (Scribner's)

GLOSSARY OF WORDS ABOUT SEEING AND BLINDNESS

Here are some words that will help you understand what it means to have a visual handicap and how people adjust to it.

blind: see *legally blind* and *visually handicapped*.

Braille: a system of writing developed by Louis Braille, a French musician and teacher who was blind himself. It uses raised dots, like bumps, on paper. A person reads by feeling with the fingers.

cane walking: a method of getting about. People with visual handicaps carry a white cane that they swing ahead of them to identify what lies ahead.

glaucoma: an eye disease that causes people to lose sight in the center of their vision.

guide dog: a dog who travels with persons having visual handicaps. The dog is trained to identify barriers and signals so its owner can walk easily.

legally blind: term referring to a person who, even with glasses or contacts, sees less at 20 feet (6 m) than a person with normal vision sees at 200 feet (61 m); also refers to someone who cannot see to the sides, who has "tunnel vision."

mobility: the ability to get from place to place.

mobility training: a method of learning how to be mobile, to get around.

orientation: knowing where you are.

orientation training: a system that teaches people who can't see to use their other senses in order to locate themselves and other objects.

sighted: having sight; being able to see.

trailing: using the back of the fingers to follow lightly over a surface. Blind people use this technique for *orientation* or to find something. It also tells them if anything is in the way.

tunnel vision: vision narrowed to the area straight ahead; also called "gun-barrel vision."

visually handicapped: also called VH; the modern word for blind. It means legal blindness.

53

INDEX

balancing 28
bike 12, 18, 22, 43
Braille blocks 31
Braille, Louis 48
Braille telephones 49
Braille watches 49
Braille writing 18, 31, 39, 48-49
bumping 9, 11, 14, 18, 39

camera 6, 10
cane 8, 49
cars 9, 14, 15, 18, 25, 34, 49
causes of blindness 11, 14, 42
color 9, 14, 26, 35, 39, 45, 48
computers 49
cruelty 45

darkness 11, 26, 35, 43, 45
dreams 9, 37
driving 9, 18-19, 25, 34

family 11, 12
flowers 46
flying 26, 34, 35
friends 6, 11, 15, 18, 21-22, 26, 31,
    40, 43

guide dog 26, 49

hearing 17, 21, 23, 26, 43, 48, 50
helping 12, 25, 39, 46, 50
holding 33
homesickness 11, 19, 37

imagination 19, 35, 43, 44, 45
independence 12, 15, 18, 23, 25,
    39, 46
isolation 43

large print 49
legal blindness 48, 49

light 9, 11, 26, 35, 48
loneliness 43

magnifiers 49
meeting a blind person 50
music 21, 34, 37, 43

night 9, 26, 37, 48

operations 11
Optacon 49
oxygen 14, 37

pictures 6, 10, 17, 19, 25, 26, 33,
    35, 39, 42, 43, 44, 45
playing 14, 17, 21-22, 28, 37, 43
pouring 18

reading 18, 31, 37, 39, 48-49
running 14, 18, 22, 28, 39, 43, 45

school 6, 11, 19, 25-26, 37, 39, 44,
    45, 46, 49
seeing 6, 9, 11, 12, 14, 15, 19, 21,
    25, 26, 34, 35, 39, 43, 44, 45
shapes 9, 19, 25, 26, 37
sighted people 11, 12, 25, 39, 40,
    48, 49
smelling 26, 32, 33, 46, 48
spelling 31
streets 12, 14, 15, 18, 23, 25, 39,
    43, 49, 50
swimming 43

Talking Books 49
tape recorder 49
tasting 26, 32
teacher 32
television 17, 19, 25, 39, 43, 45
touching 9, 10, 17, 26, 32, 33,
    39, 46, 48

traffic signals 49
TV screen enlarger 49
typewriter 49

work 12, 25, 34, 37
writing 31, 49